Frederick Nc
CLASSICAL GUITAR
TREASURY

Solo Guitar

Compiled, edited and
fingered by Frederick Noad

Chester Music
(A division of Music Sales Limited)
8/9 Frith Street, London W1V 5TZ

Introduction

The arrangements and transcriptions collected in this volume comprise
a number of works previously published in the Noad Guitar Library series,
together with some newly transcribed editions. Some, such as Dowland's
Lachrimae Pavan, or Sor's *Variations On A Theme Of Mozart* are already well established
in the concert repertoire. Others, including the de Visée *Suite In G Minor* are
less well-known and deserve wider recognition. The de Visée exhibits the strong
melodic gift well-known from his popular *D Minor Collection*.

Of the transcriptions I particularly enjoy the *Variations On A Theme of Locatelli*
by the little-known composer Joachim Bernhard Hagen, which I believe
survives well the transfer from the baroque lute and has the potential of a real
concert showpiece. To the best of my knowledge this work has not appeared in
print in this century. John Blow's *The Self-Banished Lover*, originally for voice
and lute, harpsichord or organ, is one of his best melodies and transfers well
to the guitar.

In terms of period the pieces span from the late Renaissance to the end of
the classical period. With the exception of the Handel keyboard originals and the
John Blow song, all the pieces were written for plucked stringed instruments,
including the Renaissance lute, baroque guitar and lute, and finally the six stringed
guitar of the classical period. Also included are pieces originally written for
the 'English Guitar', which was in fact the metal-strung cittern so popular in the
late 18th century.

In fact the common element in this diverse collection is perhaps to be
found in the strong melodic quality of the works, which has been a major factor
in their selection. I hope that guitarists will find something old and something
new to entertain them in this volume!

Frederick Noad

Exclusive distributors:
Music Sales Limited, Newmarket Road, Bury St. Edmunds, Suffolk IP33 3YB.

Cover by Michael Bell Design.
This book © Copyright 1998 Chester Music.
Order No. CH61466
ISBN 0-7119-6977-9

Cover image courtesy of Superstock.
Printed in Malta by Interprint Limited.

Contents

Minuet: The Self-Banished Lover

Dr. John Blow was one of the first choir boys of the Royal Chapel following the Restoration. He later became organist there, moving to Westminster Abbey following the death of Purcell in 1695. When Purcell's widow published the famous collection of his songs under the title *Orpheus Britannicus*, Blow made a similar collection of his own work: *Amphion Anglicus* (1700). It is from this book that the Minuet is taken.

Blow was sometimes bold in his harmonies, and this song exhibits some surprising chord changes reminiscent of the lutenist John Wilson. The original was for voice and organ, harpsichord or theorbo lute. It should be performed in a fluid, singing style.

John Blow (1649-1708)

Transcribed, edited and fingered by Frederick Noad

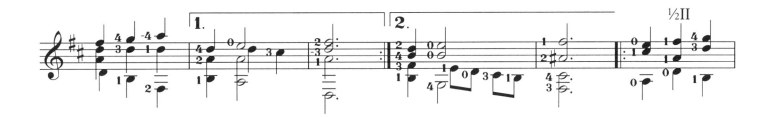

Matteo Carcassi

Matteo Carcassi was born in Florence in 1792. As a young man he established his reputation as a guitar virtuoso in his native land, and after a successful tour of Germany made his way to Paris at the age of 28. At the time the guitar world of the French capital was dominated by his older compatriot, Ferdinando Carulli, who had done much to popularise the instrument with his performances, teaching method and prolific publications. Carcassi's modern approach to melody and harmony quickly won him favour, and in 1822 he made the first of what were to become regular concert appearances in London. After a successful career as both a composer and performer he died in Paris in 1853.

Carcassi is best known for his two instructional works: the *Complete Method for the Guitar* Op.59 and its sequel 25 *Melodic and Progressive Studies* Op.60. Both works have been constantly reprinted since Carcassi's lifetime, and are probably as popular now as they were then. However, his more extended solo works have suffered almost total neglect, and the trivial short pieces that have found their way into modern anthologies are far from representative of his best work.

The three *Sonatinas* undoubtedly contributed materially to the growth of Carcassi's reputation and they are notable for the new effects he achieves. These are not the more obvious theatrical ones achieved by use of the tambour, harmonics, left hand alone, etc., but rather a greater freedom of modulation than his older compatriots Carulli and Giuliani, and a use of the higher positions demonstrating a familiarity with the full range of the fingerboard.

In spite of the use of higher positions these pieces are by no means difficult to play. The sequences are logical and fall naturally under the hand. For the student of moderate ability these works offer the opportunity to explore in more extended form the music of one of the most popular composers from the formative years of the classical guitar.

Sonatina I

Matteo Carcassi (1792-1853)
Edited and fingered by Frederick Noad

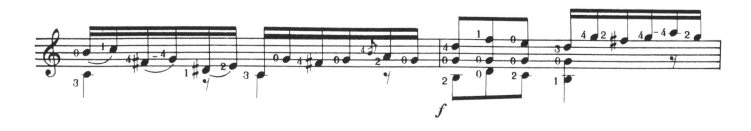

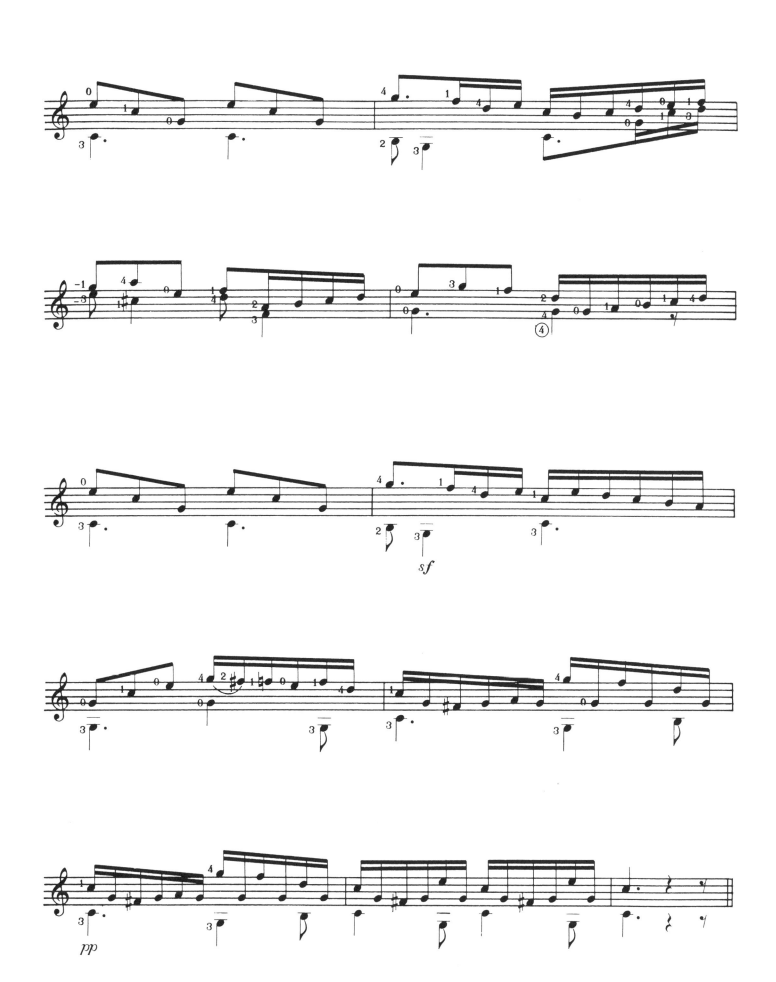

Rondo

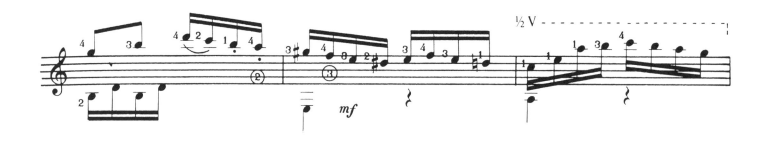

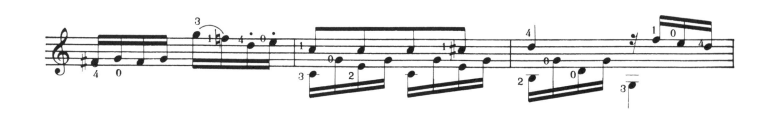

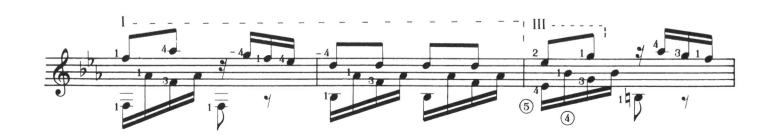

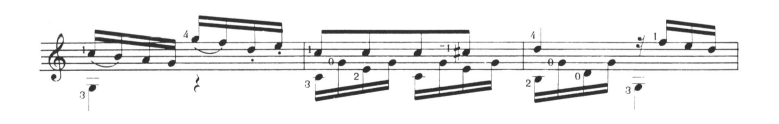

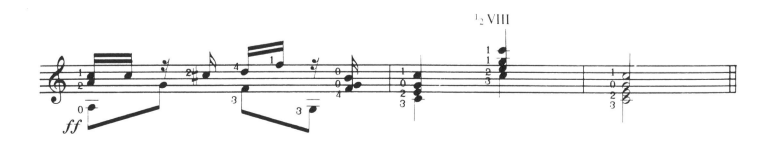

Sonatina II

Matteo Carcassi (1792-1853)
Edited and fingered by Frederick Noad

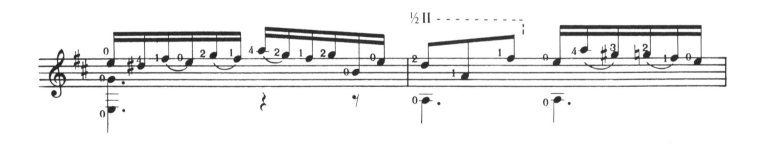

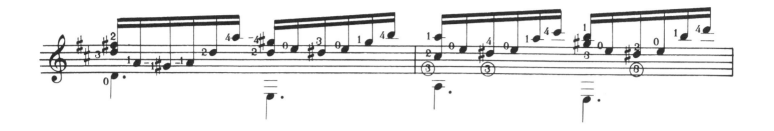
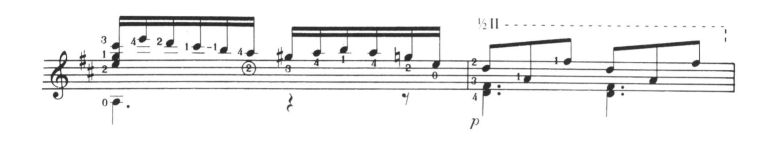

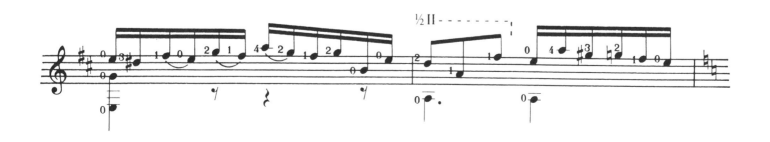

Rondo

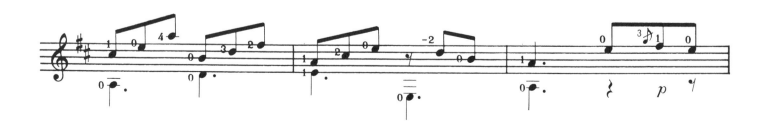

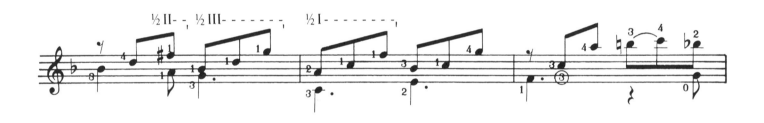

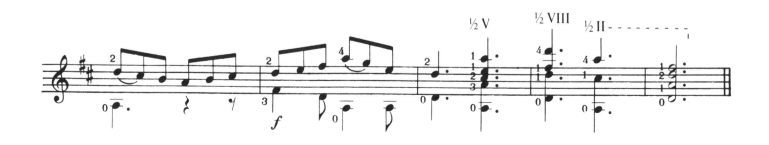

Sonatina III

Matteo Carcassi (1792-1853)
Edited and fingered by Frederick Noad

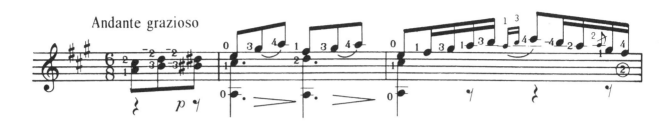

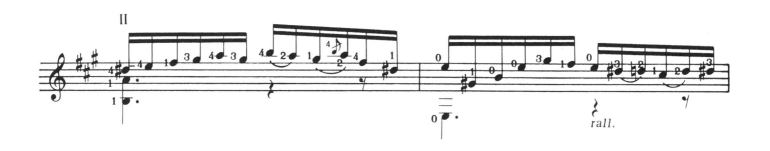

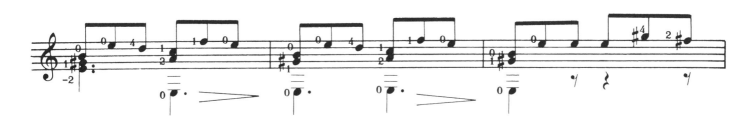

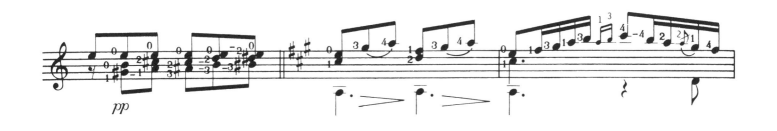

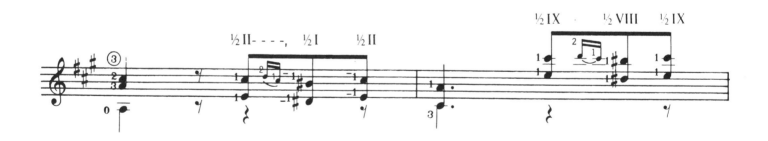

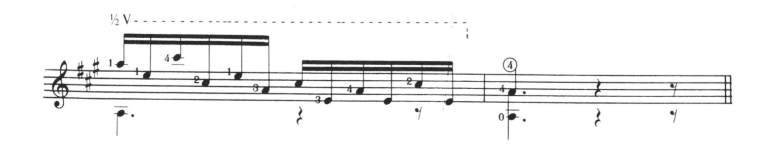

Rondo

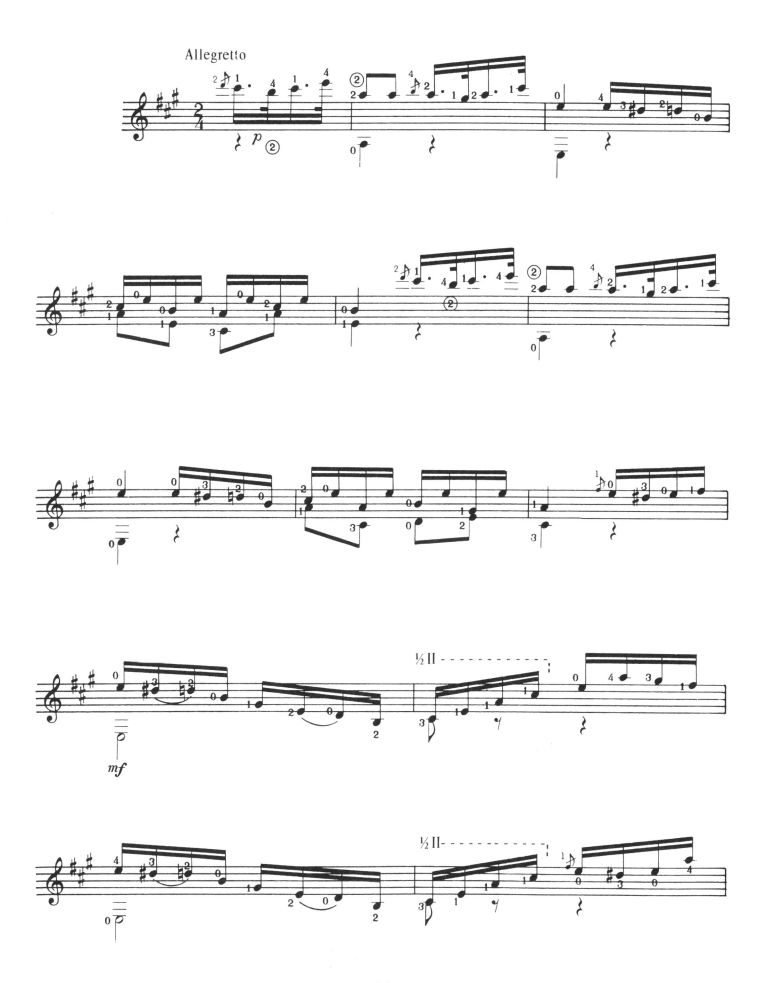

Mineur

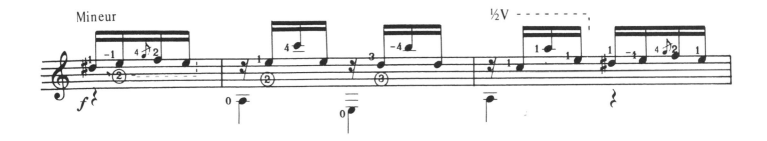

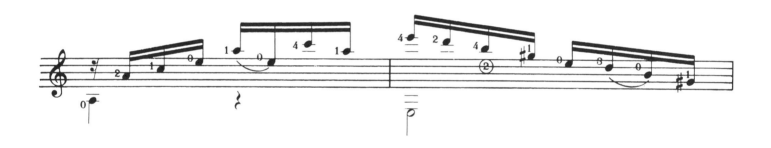

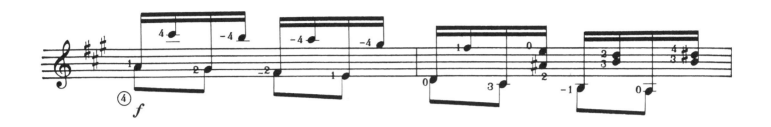

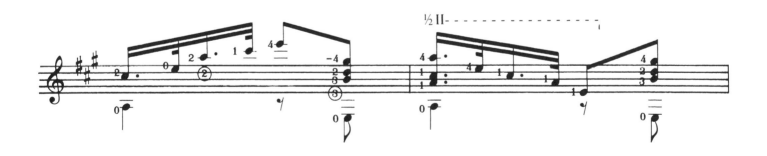

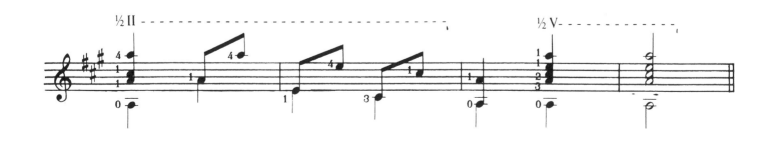

John Dowland

John Dowland (1563-1626) has been described as 'the rarest Musician that his age did behold.' A celebrated performer as well as composer, Dowland travelled extensively in Europe, and served as Lutenist to Christian IV of Denmark at a time when (possibly by reason of his religious beliefs) he was unable to obtain a post under Queen Elizabeth. Finally in 1612 he was appointed one of the King's lutes at the court of James I, a very belated recognition of a man who was by then considered the finest lutenist in Europe.

The bulk of Dowland's music for solo lute remains in manuscript form, the only substantial printed source being the *Variety of Lute Lessons* published by his son Robert in 1610. Nevertheless nearly a hundred authenticated lute pieces survive, and the music is once again attaining the extraordinary popularity that it enjoyed in Elizabethan and Jacobean times.

The following pieces are prepared primarily for guitarists, who more than any will be the performers of this music. The fingering offered is for standard guitar tuning, but more experienced players may prefer to tune the third string down a semitone to F sharp. This parallels the intervals of the lute and greatly simplifies the playing of some passages.

Complaint

John Dowland (1563-1626)
Edited and fingered by Frederick Noad

Lachrimae Pavan

John Dowland (1563-1626)
Edited and fingered by Frederick Noad

The Shoemaker's Wife

John Dowland (1563-1626)
Edited and fingered by Frederick Noad

44

The Frog Galliard

John Dowland (1563-1626)
Edited and fingered by Frederick Noad

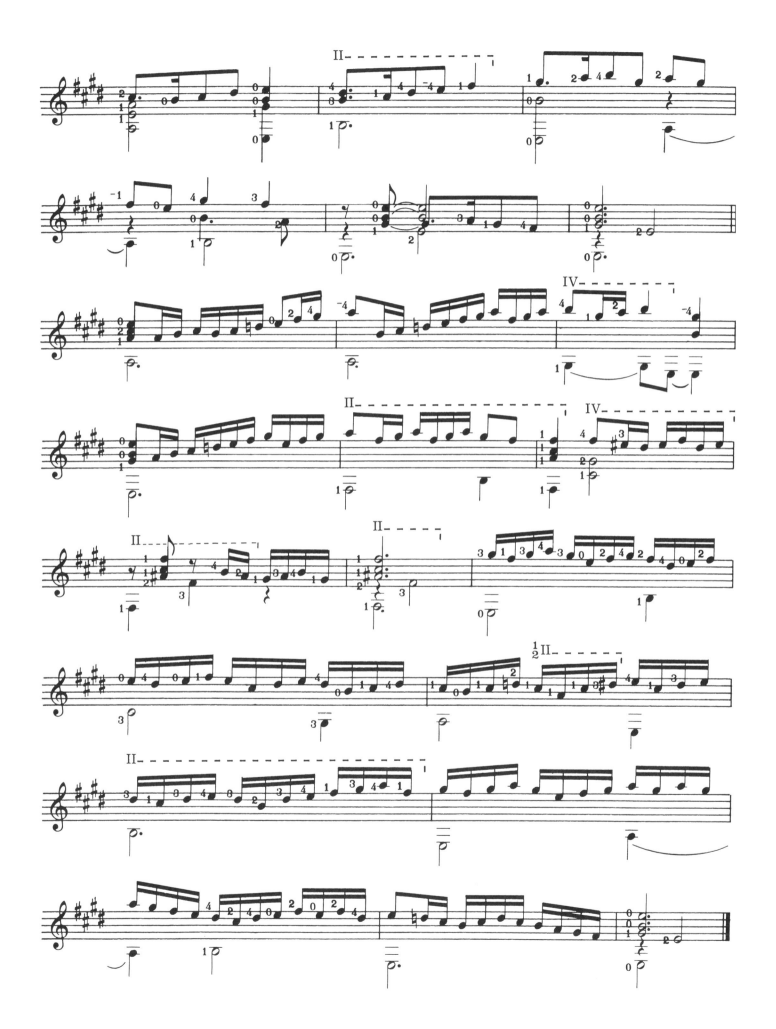

The Right Honourable The Lady Rich, Her Galliard

John Dowland (1563-1626)

Edited and fingered by Frederick Noad

Mrs White's Nothing

John Dowland (1563-1626)
Edited and fingered by Frederick Noad

Mauro Giuliani

The *Sonata in C major* Op.15 by Mauro Giuliani (1780-1829) was published in 1808, at a time when the young Italian was achieving considerable success in Vienna. He had arrived two years earlier as an unknown into a musical society which regarded the guitar merely as an instrument with which to accompany the voice. Yet in this comparatively short period his dazzling ability as a performer and the pleasing nature of his compositions had earned such comments in the musical journals as 'In truth he handles the guitar with a rare elegance, proficiency and power', and 'M. Giuliani... perhaps the leading guitarist of all up to the present day'.

This sonata is of only moderate technical difficulty, which perhaps contributes to its popularity. It is surprising, in view of this popularity, that it has been almost impossible to find a fingered edition in print that contains the complete work without arbitrary alterations and abbreviations.

The present version is based on the first publication, issued by the Imprimerie Chimique of Vienna and contains the complete score. The fingering is editorial (the original containing only an occasional indication of position) but the dynamic markings are those of the composer.

Sonata In C Major Op.15

I

Mauro Giuliani (1780-1829)
Edited and fingered by Frederick Noad

Allegro Spiritoso

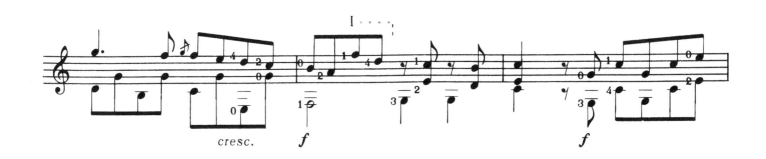

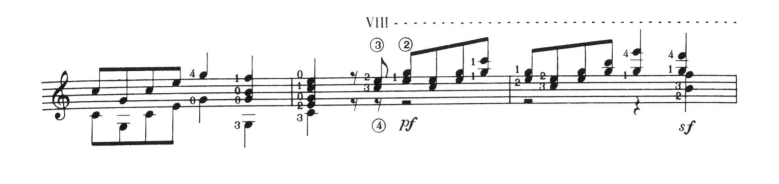

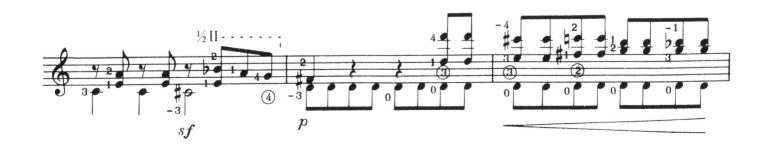

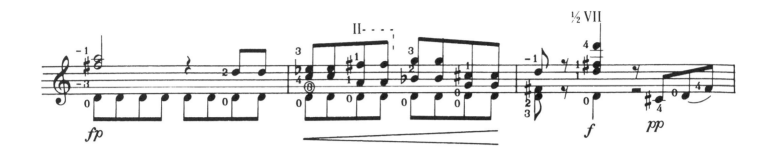

54

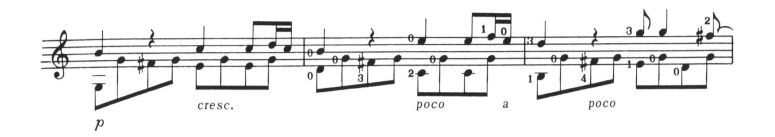

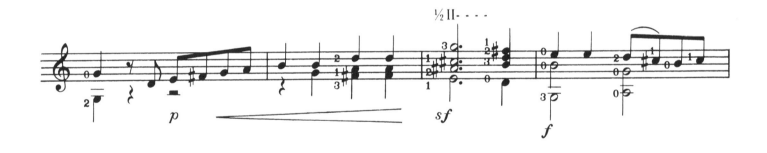

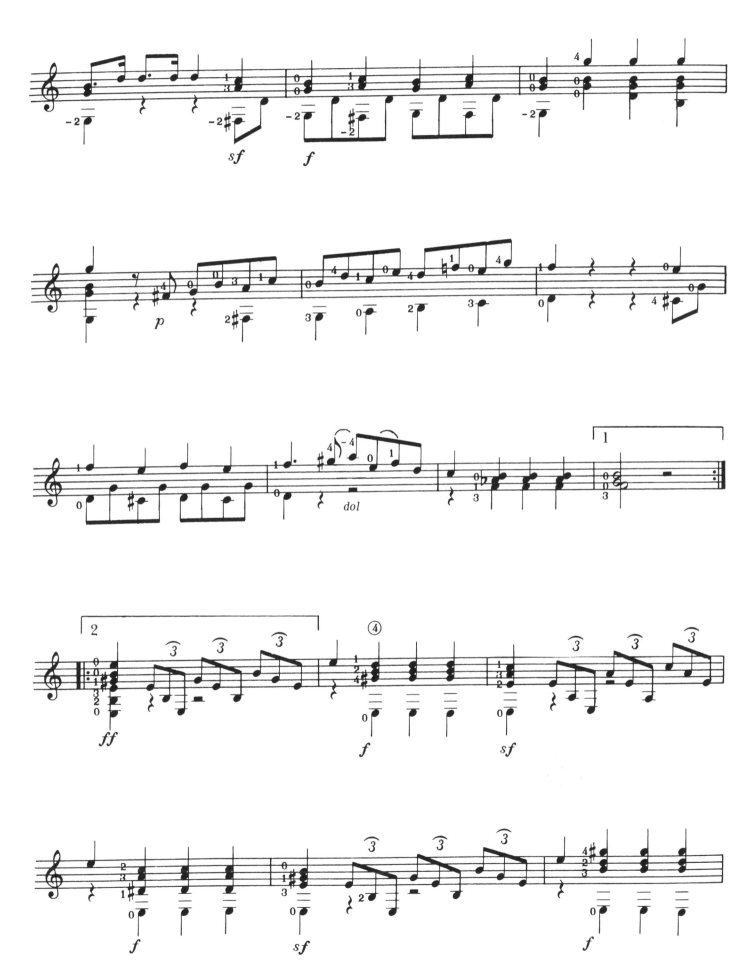

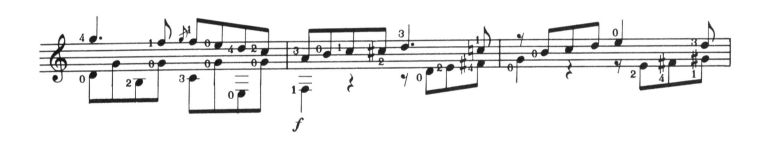

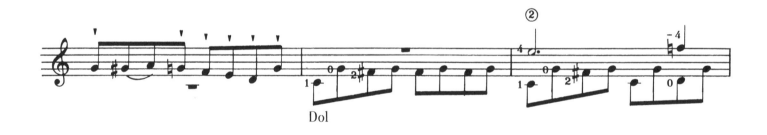

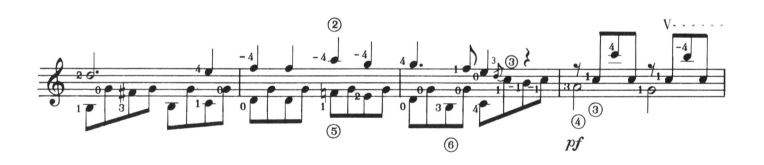

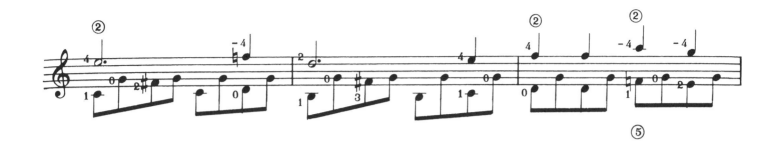

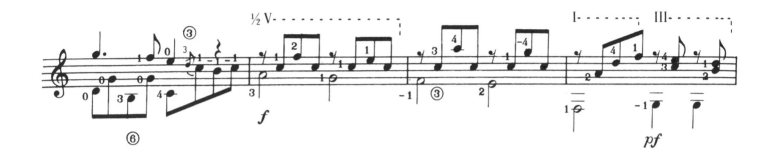

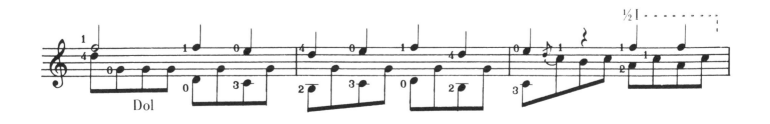

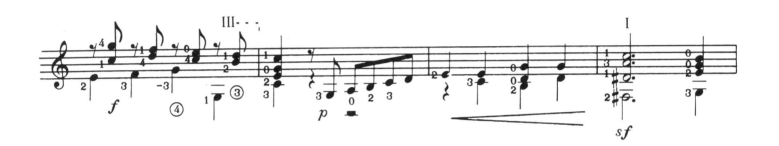

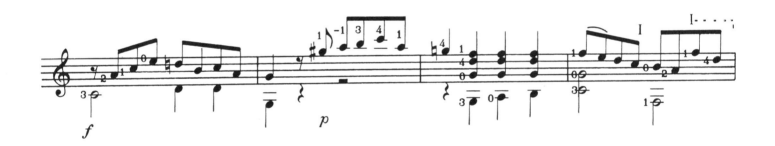

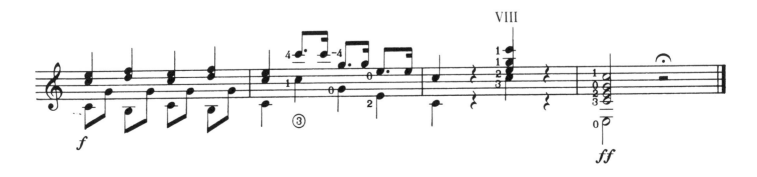

II

Adagio con grande espressione

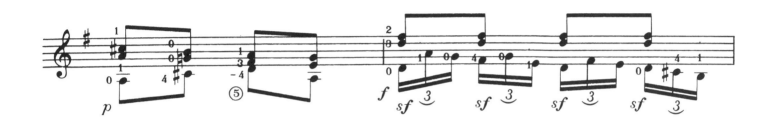

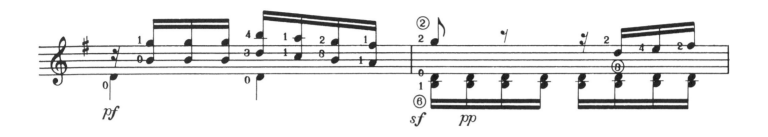

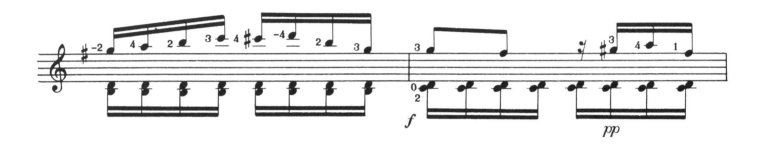

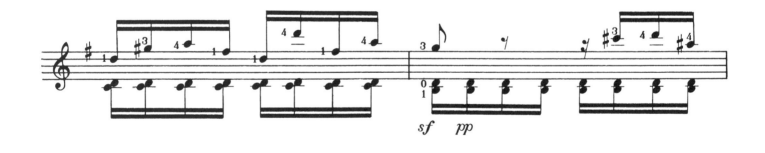

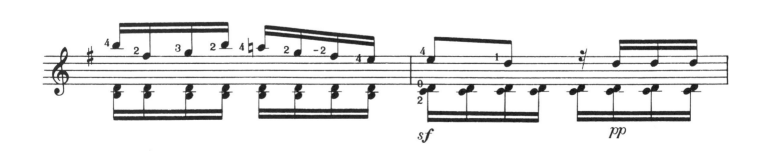

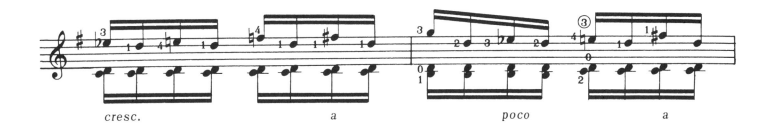

cresc.   *a*   *poco*   *a*

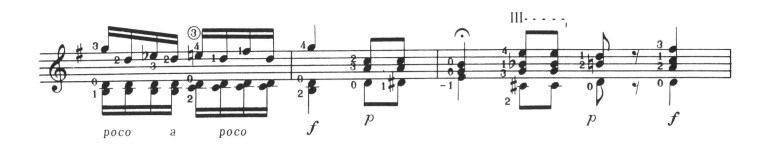

poco   *a*   *poco*   *f*   *p*   *p*   *f*

p   *sempre*

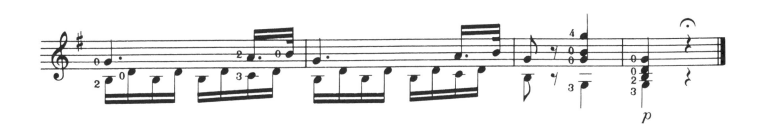

p

71

III

Allegro vivace

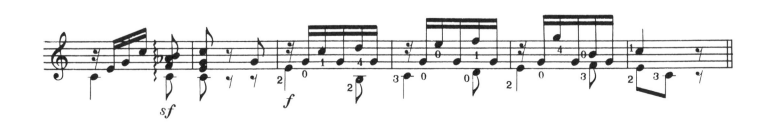

Minore

p　　　　　*sf*　　　　*sf*

slargandosi

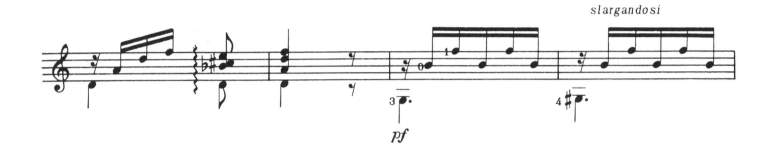

pf

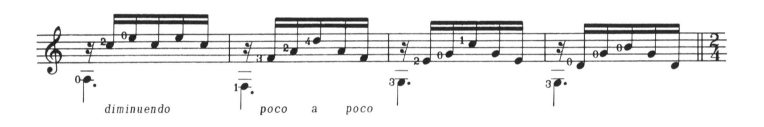

diminuendo　　*poco*　　a　　*poco*

Grazioso

mezza voce

cresc.

f　　*p*　　　　　　　　　　　　　　　　　*pp*

mezza voce

pf　　　　　　　　　　*p*

Dol

rallentando

Allegro vivace

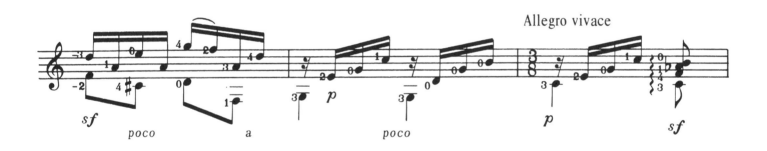

sf   *poco*   *a*   *p*   *poco*   *p*   *sf*

sf   *sf*   *f*

p   *sf*

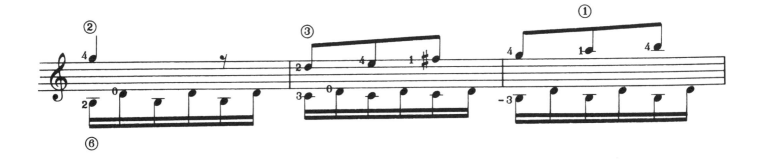

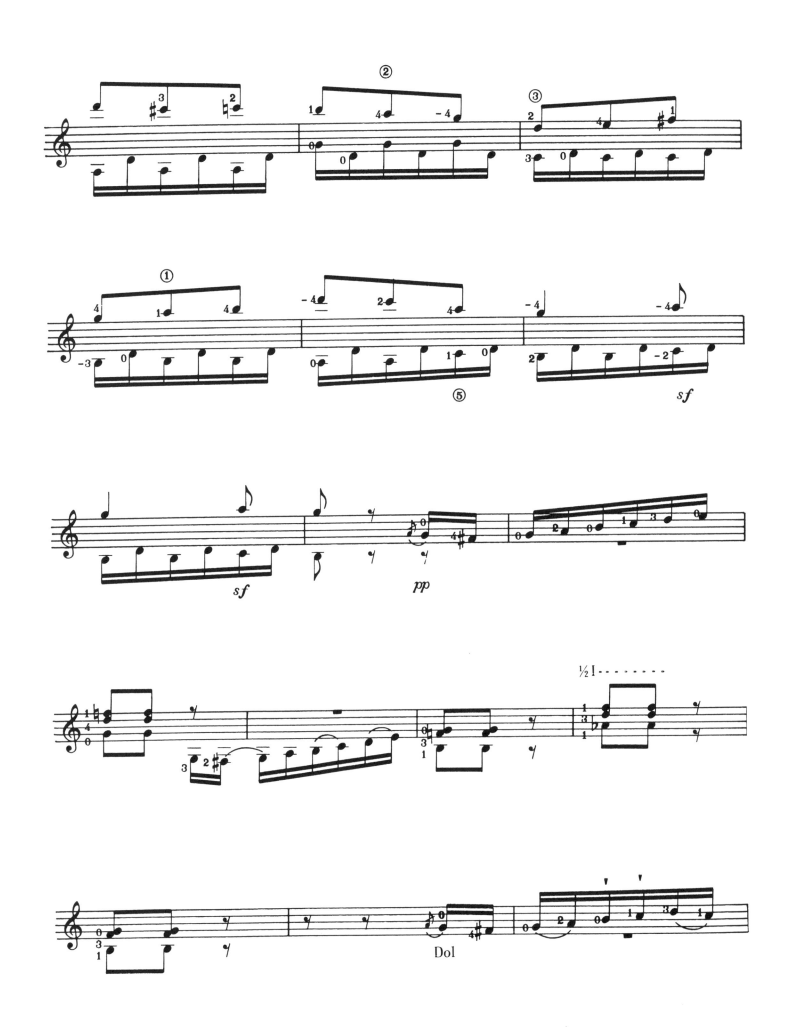

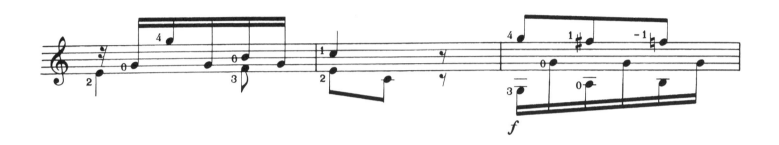

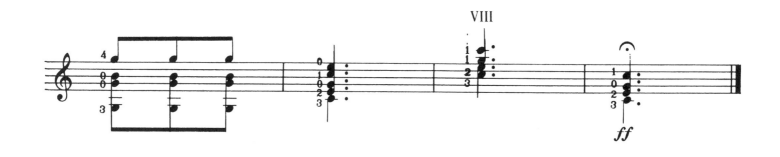

Variations On A Theme By Locatelli

In Augsberg town library in Germany there is a manuscript containing the works of the little-known lutenist Joachim Bernhard Hagen of Hamburg, from 1766 a chamber musician in Bayreuth. In it is a set of variations on a theme by the spectacular violinist Locatelli.

The work translates well to guitar, though there are a few practice spots. The first variation is particularly effective when the arpeggios are played with speed and accuracy, and the same applies to the running scales of the final variation. Variation II, with a variety of tremolo, was played on the lute by alternating between unison strings, alas not practical on the guitar. However, the repeated notes can still sound effective as a complete contrast to the other movements. Variation III calls for skillful use of tone quality and vibrato to sustain the very transparent texture.

Theme

J.B. Hagen

Transcribed, edited and fingered by Frederick Noad

Variation I

Variation II

Variation III

Variation IV

90

The following transcriptions are drawn from simple movements in Handel's trio sonatas and works for keyboard. Handel did not, as far as is known, write solo works for the lute or guitar, although he did occasionally use the theorbo-lute as an accompanying instrument. Nevertheless the simpler pieces have great charm when played on the guitar, and the transcriptions give the student the opportunity for acquaintance with one of the greatest of all musicians.

Passepied

George Frederic Handel (1685-1759)
Transcribed for guitar by Frederick Noad

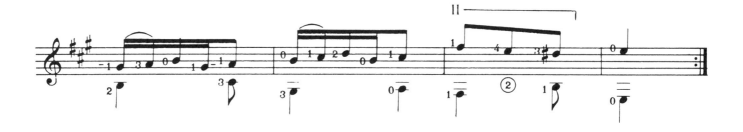

Menuet I

George Frederic Handel (1685-1759)
Transcribed for guitar by Frederick Noad

Menuet II

George Frederic Handel (1685-1759)

Transcribed for guitar by Frederick Noad

Menuet I
da Capo

Gavotte

George Frederic Handel (1685-1759)
Transcribed for guitar by Frederick Noad

Menuet

George Frederic Handel (1685-1759)
Transcribed for guitar by Frederick Noad

Sarabande

George Frederic Handel (1685-1759)
Transcribed for guitar by Frederick Noad

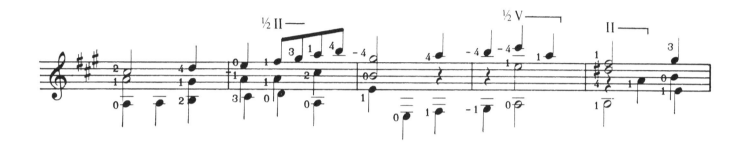

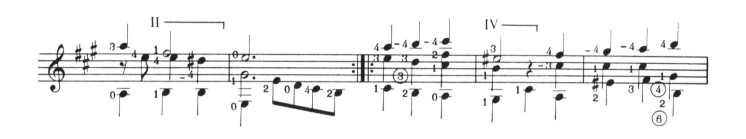

Gavotte

George Frederic Handel (1685-1759)

Transcribed for guitar by Frederick Noad

Fuga

George Frederic Handel (1685-1759)
Transcribed for guitar by Frederick Noad

6th string to D

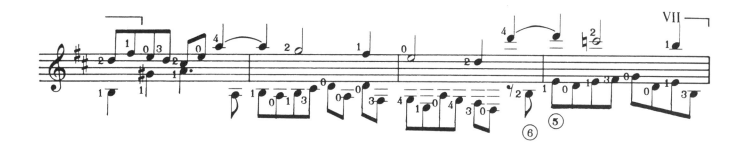

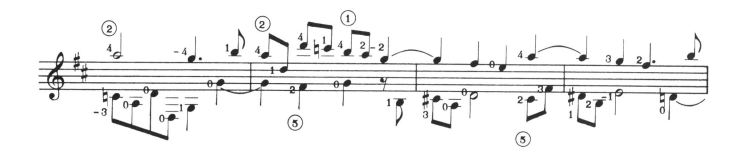

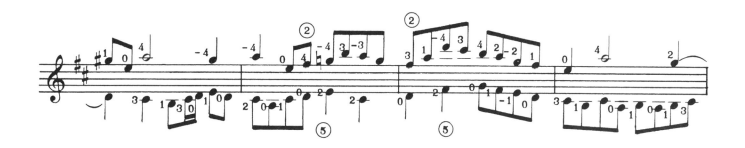

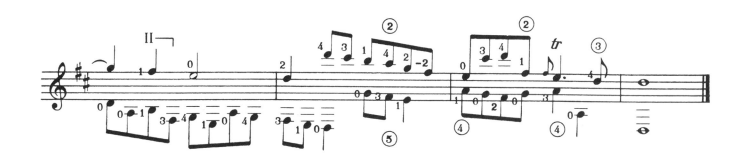

Introduction and Variations
on the Air *'Marlborough'* Op.28

The theme of this work is an 18th century French nursery song entitled 'Malbrouk S'en Va-t-en Guerre'.
It is generally supposed that 'Malbrouk' was a corruption of 'Marlborough', the reference being to the
great Duke. Although doubt has been cast on this theory due to the occurrence of the name Malbrouk in
literature of the middle ages, it is clear that the belief existed in Sor's time since his title used
the word 'Malborough' – a misspelling but close enough.

The tune is the familiar one sung to 'For He's A Jolly Good Fellow' and 'We Won't Go Home 'Til Morning'.
This edition corresponds to that of Sor's principal publisher Antoine Messonier which bore the plate
number 474. The fingering is editorial, there being none in the original.

Introduction

6th string to D

George Frederic Handel (1685-1759)

Transcribed for guitar by Frederick Noad

Theme

Variation I

Variation II

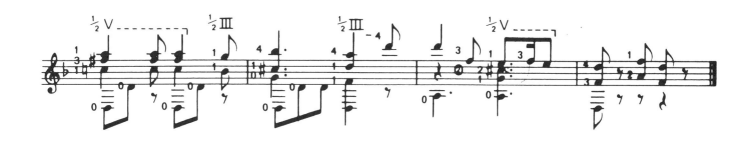

Variation III

Variation IV

Variation V

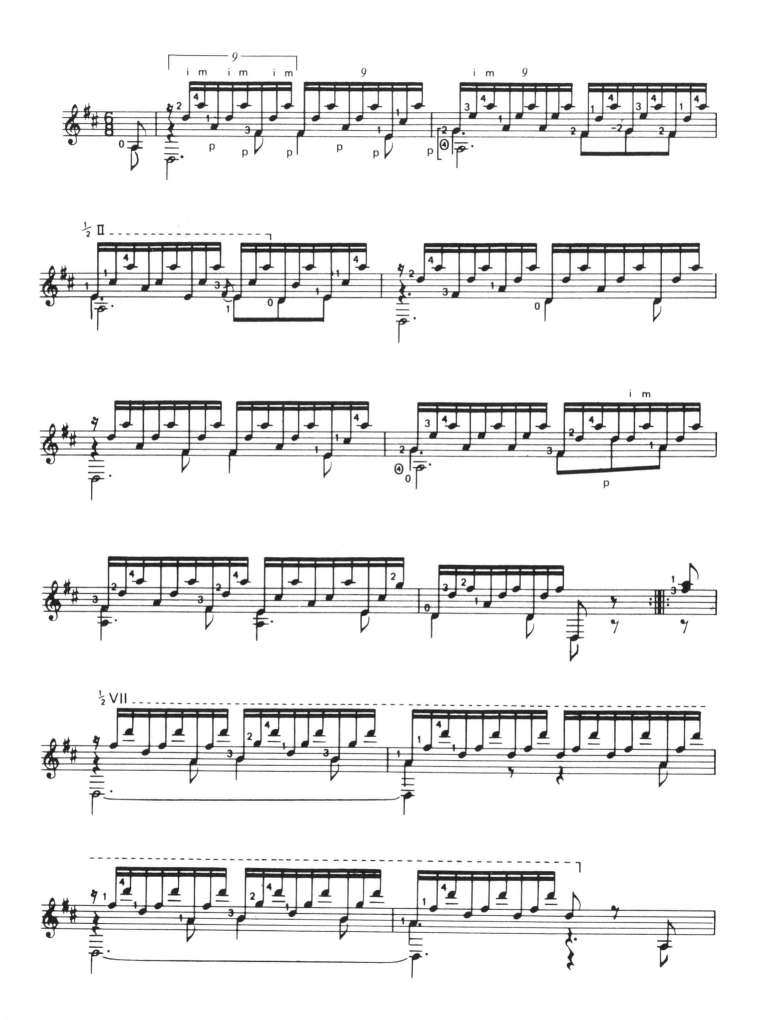

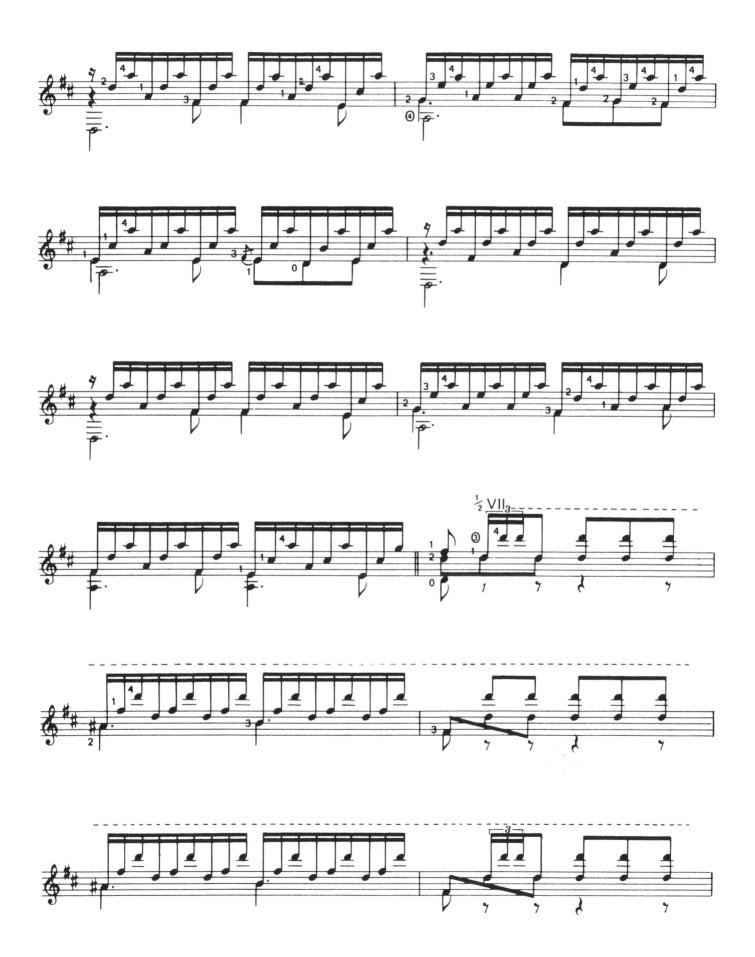

Lento a piacere

Fernando Sor

Fernando Sor (1778-1839) was the most distinguished of the early 19th century composer guitarists whose pioneer work established the guitar, with its recently added sixth string, as a solo instrument of considerable capacity. Sor was an accomplished singer, and a prolific composer of opera and ballet music. His early training took place in the celebrated school of music of the Montserrat monastery near Barcelona, and he was able to bring to his compositions for the guitar a degree of overall musicianship shared by few of his contemporaries and rivals.

The earlier compositions of Fernando Sor (Op.1-33) were collected into a principal edition by his friend and publisher Antoine Messonier, and a large proportion of these works has been readily available to the public since Sor's time. However, the later compositions (up to the final Op.63) were published under a different arrangement, with Sor retaining the proprietary rights, and from their comparative rarity it must be assumed these editions were smaller or less widely publicised. As a result many of the composer's mature works have been neglected in favour of the better known early compositions.

Elegiac Fantasy Op.59 was composed as an elegy on the death of Sor's pupil Mme Charlotte Breslay. A notice accompanying the publication contained a strong recommendation of the use of Dionisio Aguado's *Tripodion* as a means of achieving the effects demanded by the piece. This invention was a form of stand on which the guitar was placed, which purportedly allowed the guitar to resonate more freely as well as liberating the player from the necessity of supporting the instrument, thus allowing him greater dexterity.

The original edition does not distinguish between slurs and phrasing marks, so in some cases the interpretation must be decided by the player. The technical demands are not too great, and it is hoped that players will welcome this republication of this major work.

The *Variations On A Theme Of Mozart* Op.9 and *Sonata in C Major* Op.15 No.2 are based on editions published by Sor's friend and colleague Antoine Meissonier. The first Meissonier publication of the 'Variations' lacked the first variation, but a later edition published during Sor's lifetime presented the complete work in its final form. The revised Meissonier edition is identical in all important respects with the first English edition published by the Royal Harmonic Institution in 1821, which bore on the title page the words 'As performed by the Author at the Nobilities Concerts'.

The fingering is editorial apart from the very occasional indications in the original which have been preserved. The slurring appears to have been somewhat careless, being at times suggested at the beginning of a particular figure but not carried through for repetitions which obviously required the same treatment. Obvious omissions have been corrected, but additional slurs for which there is no specific evidence have been drawn above the beam to distinguish them from those of the original publication which link the note-heads in the conventional manner.

Both compositions have achieved great popularity, representing the best work of the 19th century's most distinguished composer for the guitar.

Elegiac Fantasy Op.59

Fernando Sor (1778-1839)
Edited and fingered by Frederick Noad

INTRODUCTION
Andante largo

Left hand alone...

Both hands

112

Variations On A Theme Of Mozart Op.9

Fernando Sor (1778-1839)
Edited and fingered by Frederick Noad

Andante moderato

Pour la 2ᵐᵉ fois

122

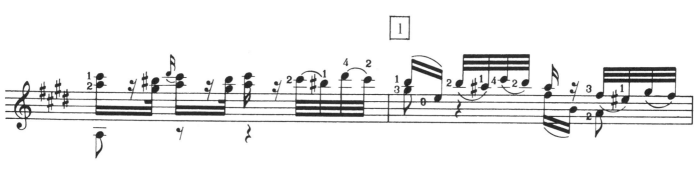

1   Original

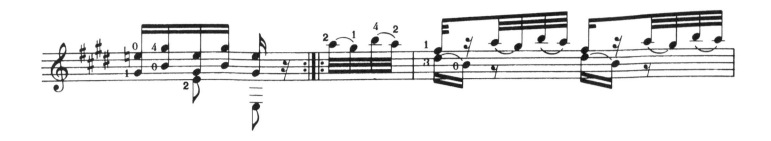

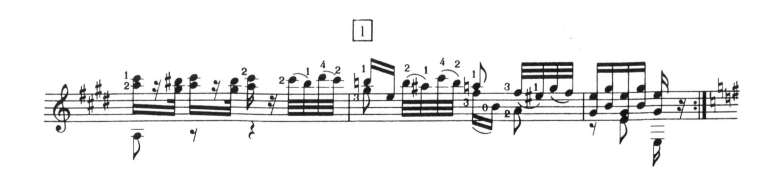

Mineur

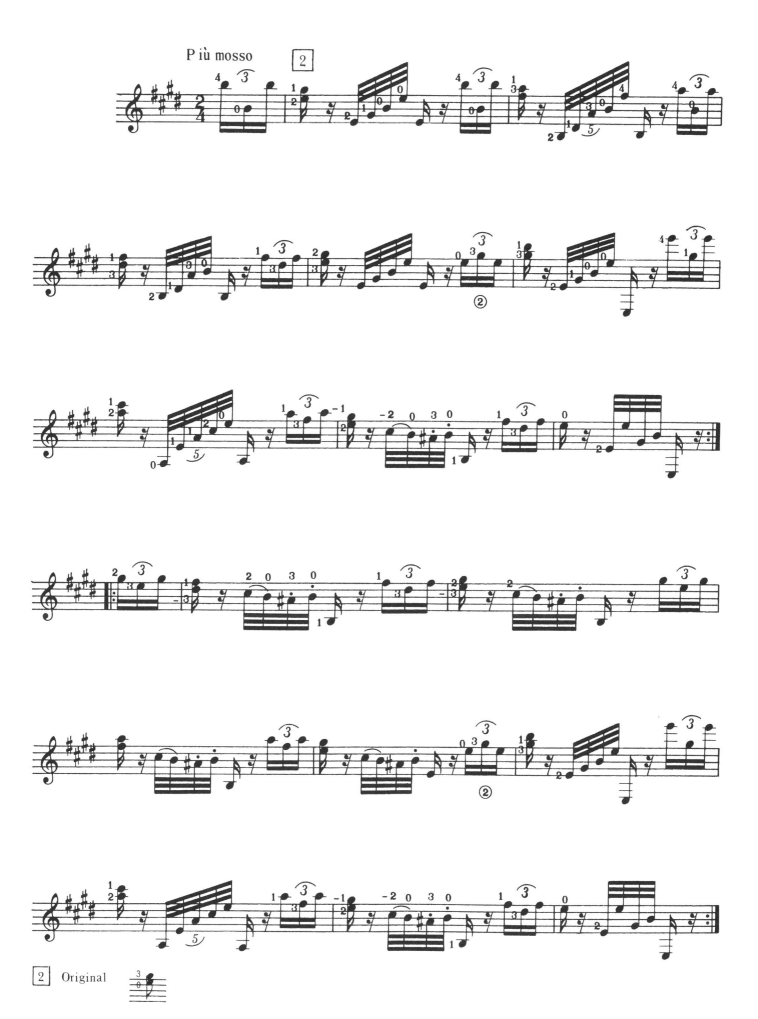

Più mosso

2 Original

127

3 I have fingered this passage assuming the triplet groups to be slurred.   Some players prefer to play one of the two scales *staccato* for contrast.

130

Sonata In C Major Op.15 No.2

Fernando Sor (1778-1839)
Edited and fingered by Frederick Noad

Allegro moderato

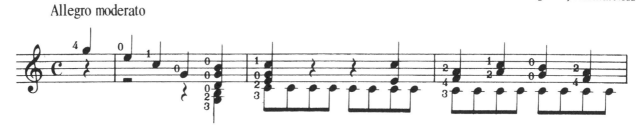

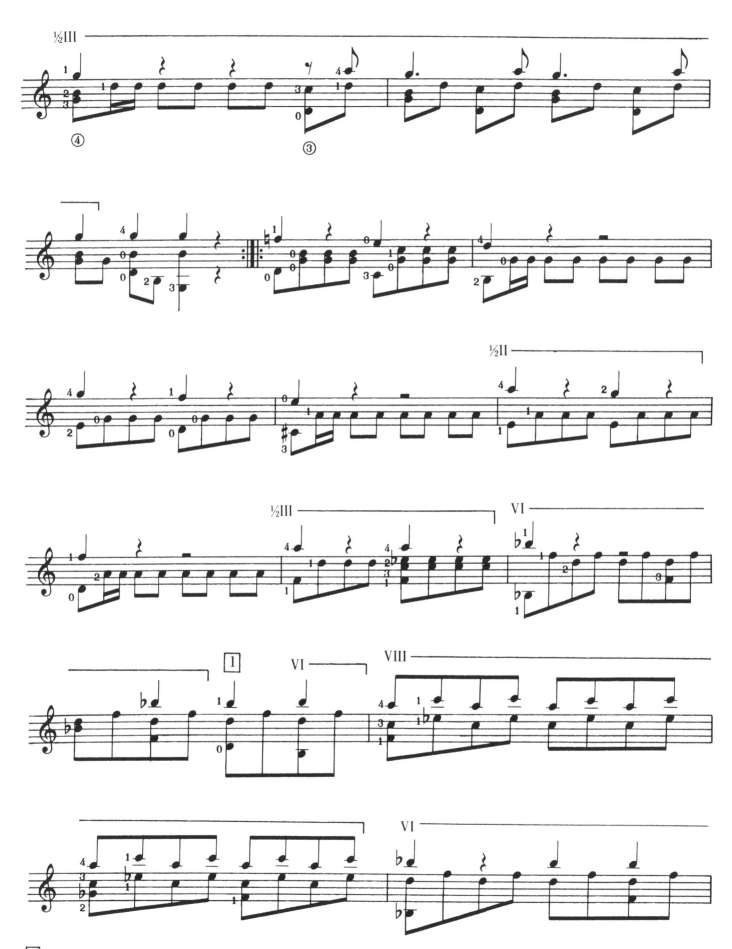

[1] Sor would undoubtedly have fingered the bass D on the 6th string with the 4th finger, thereby maintaining the bar. On the larger modern fingerboard this is considered impratical.

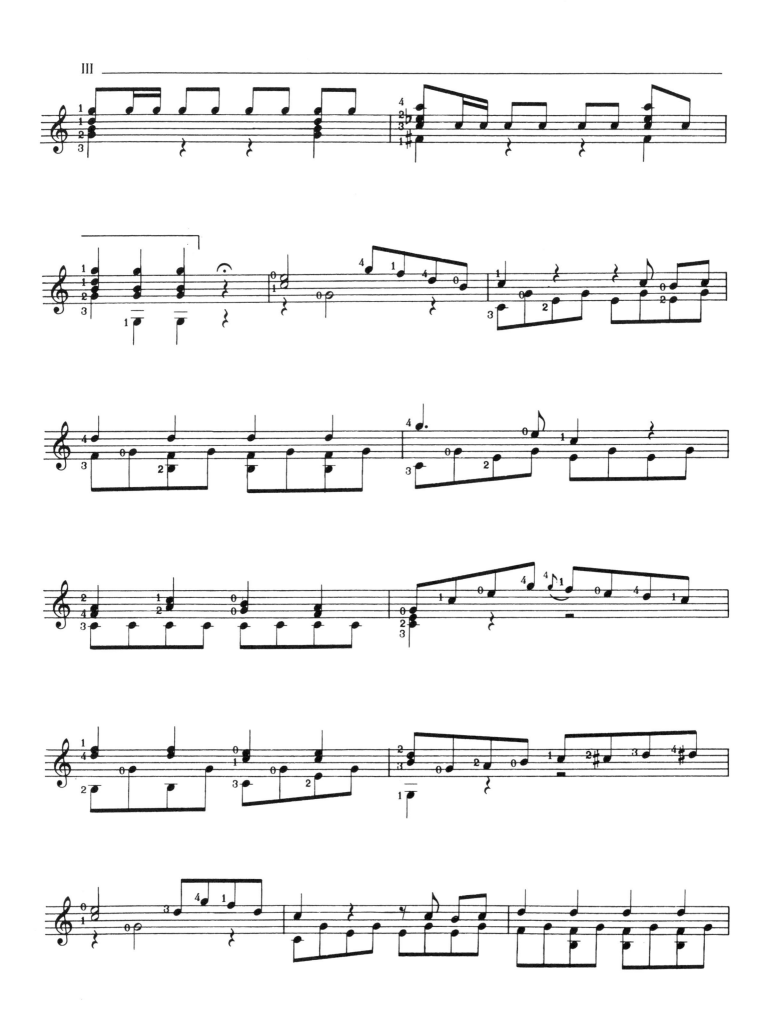

Robert de Visée

Robert de Visée (c. 1650-1725) was a performer of both the guitar and lute, and a respected chamber musician at the dazzling court of Louis XIV. His known published works consist of two books for the baroque (five course) guitar published in 1682 and 1686, and a large collection entitled *Pièces de Théorbe et de Luth* published in 1716. Unlike the guitar books which were in tablature, this final collection was written on two staves, consisting of a melody and a figured bass. Notwithstanding the title, de Visée tells us in the introduction that the collection is intended for the combination of violin, keyboard and viol.

The style of his pieces is by design similar to that of Lully, the principal figure at court and himself a guitarist at least in his private moments. The decline in interest in music for the guitar and lute which occurred in the 18th century left de Visée's music in obscurity until, over a century after his death, the guitarist Napolean Coste rediscovered the works and published an edition of his *Suite in D Minor* from the 1686 book. Since then this same suite has been constantly republished by various editors.

The *Suite In G Minor* is arranged principally from the 1716 collection, but with close reference to the parallel works in guitar tablature. The reason for using the notation rather than the tablature as a prime source is that the true bass line is clearly expressed. In the guitar versions the bass is frequently altered or simplified to accommodate the smaller range of the five-course guitar. In justifying this accommodation de Visée wrote in the introduction to his 1682 book that 'C'est l'instrument qui le veut' – the instrument itself demands it.

The present edition is designed to take advantage of the greater range of the modern guitar, and thus preserves as far as possible the intention of the 1716 version. Where this has seemed impractical the solutions have been followed that de Visée himself used in simplifying the music for the guitar. For the many trills of short duration the following is most effective:

The pieces themselves are not difficult and demonstrate de Visée's strong melodic gift. Longer cadential trills will naturally require more extension according to the tempo of the piece.

Suite In G Minor
1. Allemand

Robert de Visée (c.1650-1725)
Transcribed, edited and fingered by Frederick Noad

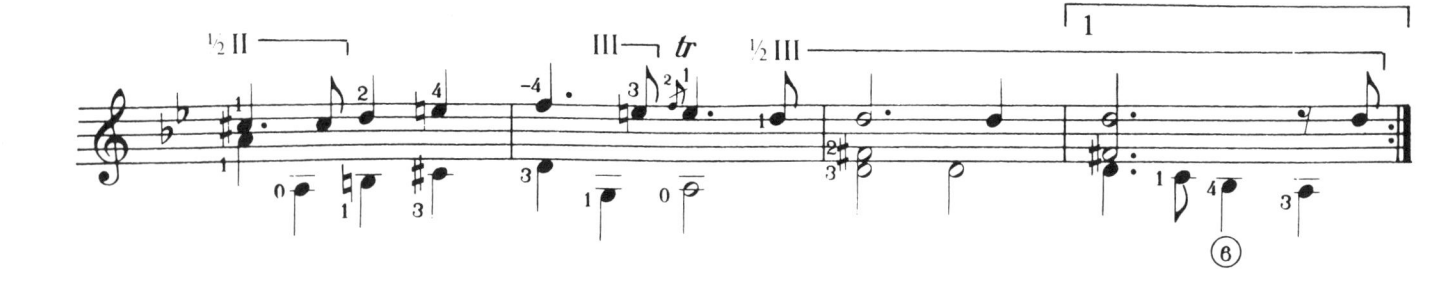

2. Courante

3. Sarabande

4. Gavotte

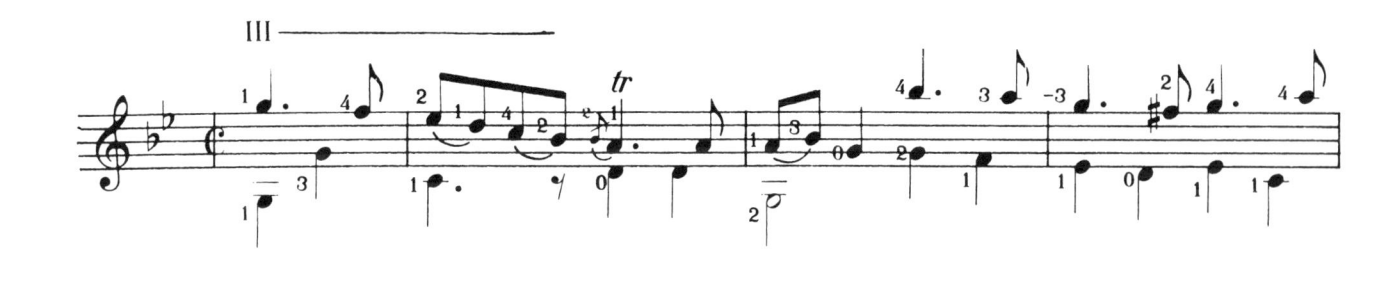

5. Menuet

6. Pastorale

7. Gigue